Give Me Half !

I have one whole pizza . . . and it's all for me!

I'm going to get some pizza—just you wait and see.

I know you want some pizza, Sis.
You only get one slice.

You'd better give me more than that.
Why can't you be nice?

You have to share the pizza. It must be split in two.
The pieces should be cut the same for each of you.

and make

1 half pizza and 1 half pizza make 1 whole pizza.

$$\frac{1}{2} \text{ and } \frac{1}{2} \text{ is } 1$$

$$\frac{1}{2} + \frac{1}{2} = 1$$

What is that behind her back?
The last can of juice, I think.

If he takes some juice from me,
I won't have much to drink.

I gave you half of mine, so you must share yours, too.

I'll give you just a sip, but not until I'm through.

Split the juice in half. Again, you have to share.
And when you pour it out,
make sure that you pour fair.

and make $\frac{}{}$ juice

1 half can of juice and 1 half can of juice
make 1 whole can of juice.

$\frac{1}{2}$ and $\frac{1}{2}$ is 1

$\frac{1}{2} + \frac{1}{2} = 1$

BUDDY

I know she has some cupcakes.
I saw her with a pack.

I'm going to hide my cupcakes
and save them for a snack.

Hey, what's that on your chair?
You'd better give me some!

I'm going to eat them both myself
and leave you just a crumb.

Your cupcakes must be shared—and do I need repeat?
You both get half the pack.
And don't you two dare cheat!

1 cupcake and 1 cupcake make a pack of 2 cupcakes.

1 and 1 is 2

1 + 1 = 2

1 is ½ of 2

I have a stack of biscuits –
and you get just one bite.

You'd better give me half that stack,
or else I'll start a fight!

Hey . . . WAIT!

Too late!

There are biscuits on the floor.
There's pizza everywhere.

There's juice spilled on the table
and sticky stuff under my chair.

We're going to be in trouble.
We've made a great big mess!
But I have made no more than you,
and you have made no less.

We'd better each clean half.
There's so much work to do.
We'll be done in half the time . . .

if Buddy helps us too.

ACTIVITIES AT SCHOOL

The following activities will help you to extend children's understanding of the concepts presented in *Give Me Half*:

- Read the story asking questions throughout, such as, 'What happens when you share one whole pizza with another person?', 'How much pizza will you get?' and 'How should the pizza be cut if it is to be shared fairly?'

- Encourage the children to retell the story using the mathematical vocabulary 'half', 'whole', 'share', etc. Introduce the word 'divide' by saying that each item is 'divided equally'.

- Using pieces of paper in a variety of shapes and sizes, challenge the children to find different ways to fold them in half.

- Make a collection of different leaves and use a felt pen to show how they can be divided in half.

ACTIVITIES AT HOME

If you would like to have fun with the maths concepts presented in *Give Me Half*, here are a few suggestions:

• Read the story with your child and ask him or her to describe what is happening in each picture.

• Together draw some pizzas, drink cans, cakes and biscuits, or draw a family meal or imaginary picnic. Then cut or make lines on the drawings to show how they would be divided when sharing with another person.

• When cooking together, look at the ingredients of a recipe. Talk about how you could divide those ingredients to find half.

• Find things around the house that demonstrate halves, for example, show how shirts and trousers can be folded in half. Show that one sock, shoe or glove is half of a pair.